RESPONDING TO THE
HOLY SPIRIT

BY NANCY DUFRESNE

Responding to the Holy Spirit
Copyright © 2005 by Ed Dufresne Ministries

All Rights Reserved

ISBN: 0-940763-22-2

Published by:
Ed Dufresne Ministeries
P.O. Box 1010
Murrieta, CA 92564
www.eddufresne.org

Printed in the United States of America.

DEDICATION

Through the years, I have been privileged to observe the life of a man who has taught me the most about responding to and following the person of the Holy Spirit. His accuracy in the Spirit is keen, proficient, and is an example to be followed. It's to him, my husband, I dedicate this book.

TABLE OF CONTENTS

INTRODUCTION

I introduce this book by quoting some of those who were mightily used of God, and whose lives and ministries were marked by the moving of the Holy Spirit and the flow of the supernatural. Each statement made is a sermon that preaches volumes.

*****

"Only one thing will meet the needs of the people, and that is for you to be immersed in the life of God."
(Smith Wigglesworth)

*****

"If you find me on the street or anywhere else, if I am alone, I will be talking to God. I make it my business to talk to God all the time. If I wake in the night, I make it my business to pray. I believe that's the reason God keeps me right, always right, always ready."
(Smith Wigglesworth)

*****

"I see anything not done in the Spirit as failure."
(Smith Wigglesworth)

*****

"When the number of disciples began to multiply, the twelve had to make a definite decision not to occupy themselves with serving tables, but to give themselves continually to prayer and the ministry of the Word" (Acts 6). (Smith Wigglesworth)

"I have revival everywhere I go because I live full of the Spirit." (Smith Wigglesworth)

*****

"Nothing is impossible to a man filled with the Holy Spirit." (Smith Wigglesworth)

*****

"Being filled with the Spirit is worthwhile, no matter what it costs!" (Smith Wigglesworth)

*****

"I find nothing in the Bible but holiness, and nothing in the world but worldliness. Therefore, if I live in the world, I will become worldly; on the other hand, if I live in the Bible, I will become holy."
(Smith Wigglesworth)

*****

"The key to having miracles is hunger; but people have to be taught to be hungry." (Kenneth Hagin)

*****

"The more affluent you become, the more time you must spend with God to stay humble and focused on God." (Jeanne Wilkerson)

*****

"When you stay focused on God, then you become a magnet that draws everything to you that you will ever need." (Pat Harrison)

"Faith will do whatever it takes to get the job done."
(Ed Dufresne)

*****

"Speaking in tongues is the door to the supernatural." (J.R. Goodwin)

*****

As we launch into this study on how to respond to the Holy Spirit, I'm reminded of something the Spirit of God spoke to my heart. "Many have lost their anointing because they quit starting their day with Me. Many look upon a man who succumbed to sin and think it's that sin which caused him to fall, but their failure began when they failed to start their day with Me."

I'm struck by the amazing similarities I find in the lives of the mighty men of God who blessed their generation and impacted this earth. These spiritual giants bore lasting fruit, leaving behind a spiritual inheritance and imparted mighty revelations to bless future generations. The following elements stand out as common denominators in their spiritual lives:

1.   They lived full of the Spirit. They gave great amounts of time daily to their fellowship with God.

2.   They gave their all to God's plan for their lives every day. They gave themselves wholly to God's purpose for them and to their assignments. They lived obedient to the heavenly vision.

3.   They kept themselves free from the entanglements of this world. They didn't allow the natural affairs of daily life to take precedence over their supernatural lives in the Spirit.

Jesus was the supreme example of a life lived in the Spirit. He faced great obstacles and opposition, but lived in total, undisturbed peace, absolute victory, and continual communion with the Father.

For thirty years He prepared, and in three years He fulfilled all. All that the prophets of old had foretold of Him was accomplished in that short span of time. By the power of the Holy Spirit, who descended upon Him in the form of a dove, He lived out the Father's plan, then was raised to the right hand of the Father where He carries on His present-day ministry.

As Jesus showed us, living in the Spirit is the only way we can ever accomplish living in its highest sense and purpose.

As you continue to study, may you walk further into all that is available to you by *Responding to the Holy Spirit.*

CHAPTER ONE

Responding to the Holy Spirit

Sometime ago, my husband made a statement during the course of a sermon that stood out and seemed to follow me for months. He stated, "The reason people don't receive more in a service is because they don't respond more."

This statement planted and unlocked some things in my spirit that God expanded in me, and continues to develop in me.

In March of 2003, our church in Murrieta, California, had the privilege of hosting a crusade with Kenneth Hagin. We had just moved into our new building and the church family was working hard to finalize all the details you have when occupying a new building.

But a few months before the crusade, we reminded the congregation that we must not only prepare the building for the meetings, but we were to prepare spiritually to fully cooperate with God's plan for the crusade. I had begun teaching on how to pray for the minister and the meetings, and we had spent time praying for them.

But as we continued to pray, God began dealing with me about preparing our congregation in an additional direction. God spoke to me about the crusade saying, "You can pray for My plan to come to pass and for the Spirit of God to move, but if the people don't respond to the Spirit when He does move, it won't matter that you prayed."

I saw that as we increase our praying, we must also increase our response to the Spirit of God. I saw that the people needed more teaching on how to properly respond to the Spirit. No church service can reach its fullest potential and highest flow without the proper response of the congregation.

Sometimes ministers can become impatient with a congregation for not responding in a service as they should, but people must be taught to respond right. No one is born knowing how to respond properly; they must be taught.

If you go into a store and see a young child laying on the floor, kicking and screaming because their parent wouldn't let them have a toy they wanted, you are seeing a child who hasn't been taught how to respond properly. That child is being taught that improper response will get him his way. Not only is the child doing something wrong, but the parent is wrong in not teaching their child to respond properly.

Well, ministers can be guilty as well by assuming that congregation members should know how to respond properly to the Word and to the moving of the Holy Spirit when they haven't yet been taught.

As any parent knows, you don't teach a child something just once. You must often restate yourself over and over to them until your instruction to them becomes a part of their behavior. Likewise, a pastor must continually restate his instruction to the congregation over and over until it becomes part of their lives.

This is what the Spirit of God was showing us as we prepared for the crusade for Brother Hagin. We were going to have to teach the people how to respond properly.

When we took the time to teach the people how to respond to the Spirit of God in a service, it made all the difference in our congregation and in our services. It completely changed every service we had. Once the people were properly taught, they were eager to respond. It brought us into a whole new place in the anointing and flow of God.

Taught to Respond

In 1 Samuel 3 we read the account of Samuel, who was taken as a child by his mother, to serve in the temple under Eli the prophet.

As Samuel was laying in his bed one night, the Lord called Samuel by name. Samuel heard it but thought that Eli was calling him, so he ran to see him. Eli denied that he had called him and sent him back to lie down. After he returned to his bed, again he heard his name called and ran to Eli.

This happened three times, then Eli perceived that it was the Lord who was calling him. Eli then instructed Samuel how to respond if he was to hear his name called again.

He told him:

...Go, lie down: and it shall be, if he call thee, that thou shalt say, Speak, Lord; for thy servant heareth.

(1 Samuel 3:9)

As Samuel returned to his bed, the Lord did call his name again.

1 Samuel 3:10 reads:

And the Lord came, and stood, and called AS AT OTHER TIMES, Samuel, Samuel. Then Samuel answered, Speak; for thy servant heareth.

The Amplified Bible says that Samuel's response was, *"...Speak, Lord, for Your servant is LISTENING."*

Notice that this passage tells us that the Lord had called him at other times, but Samuel had not been taught how to hear or respond to the Lord until this occasion. People must be taught how to respond to the Lord.

Although the Lord had called Samuel's name, He didn't go any further in speaking to him until Samuel responded the right way. Note that Samuel did respond when he heard his name – he ran to Eli – but that was the wrong response.

There are many things that God would say to us or do for us if we would respond to Him the right way. A wrong response hinders us from receiving more of what God has for us. He had more to say to Samuel, but He could not continue speaking further to him until He received a response of agreement from Samuel.

Someone may wonder why God doesn't go ahead and move for someone or speak something to them, even if they haven't responded right to Him. The reason is that God won't violate our will. He won't push anything off on anyone. He will never drive or force someone to do something. That's how the enemy operates, but not God! God endeavors to lead people in the direction He has for them, but He will never force or drive them.

Therefore, He had to wait for Samuel's response of agreement before He could proceed further with the message that He had for Samuel.

Eli instructed Samuel to say, *"...Speak, Lord, for Your servant is LISTENING."* Notice that you must be listening, or giving your attention to God, if you're going to receive more from Him. Many don't take the time to listen to God, yet wonder why they don't hear Him.

Take time to listen to the Lord. No one wants to speak to someone who won't take the time to listen to them. Christians are too busy with natural things, and are neglecting to give proper time to listening to the Lord or to His Word. People who don't take the time to listen will not hear. It's not that God isn't speaking, but many aren't listening, so they don't hear what God has to say to them and they miss the mark.

In Isaiah 6:8 & 9 we read:

Also, I heard the voice of the Lord, saying, Whom shall I send, and who will go for us? Then said I (Isaiah), *Here am I; send me.*

And he said, Go...

This passage tells us that God was sending out a call in the realm of the Spirit and Isaiah heard it, and responded correctly; so God gave him further instructions to, *"Go,"* and then gives Isaiah the message to speak.

One could get the idea that possibly God wasn't singling out just Isaiah to call him, but to anyone who may have been listening for God's voice.

If Isaiah had not been listening and had not responded correctly, he would not have been sent.

God can place a call on a person's life, but if they don't respond to it correctly, He can't bring it to pass.

GOD NEEDS YOUR RESPONSE

Let's look at Mary, the mother of Jesus. The angel Gabriel appeared to her and told her that she was to give birth to a son and she was to call Him Jesus.

16

Her response to the angel was:

...be it unto me according to thy word. And the angel departed from her.

(Luke 1:38)

Mary responded right to the angel, and so God was able to bring to pass the birth of Jesus.

If God could do anything anytime He wanted, without the permission of people, like some people mistakenly believe, then why would He even bother to inform Mary about the birth of Jesus? Why didn't He just go ahead with His plan without speaking to her about it first? Because He needed her agreement to bring something to pass in her life. God doesn't force His will upon anyone – they must agree to it before He can bring it to pass.

I'm so thankful that Mary responded correctly to the angel's visit. All the earth was changed because one young woman responded right to heaven's plan. Deliverance came to the human race because Mary responded correctly to God.

Blessings can come to many when we respond right to God; but great difficulty and harm can come when we fail to respond correctly to God and His plan for our lives.

How did Mary respond? She spoke words – words that agreed with God's plan.

In contrast, let's look at Zachariah, the father of John the Baptist. An angel appeared to him and told him of the soon-coming birth of his son that he was to call John. Zachariah started asking questions of doubt instead of agreeing with the angel, and he was struck dumb, unable to speak for a season, so that he couldn't speak further and abort the plan of God.

Only when Zachariah wrote words on a tablet at John's birth saying, *"His name is John,"* was God able to loose Zachariah's tongue, for now his words agreed with God's words.

WRONG QUESTIONS PARENT UNBELIEF

When God speaks to us, we must respond correctly if what He says is to be fulfilled. If someone responded like Zachariah and began to question God's Word, God is hindered from bringing His plan to pass. To ask the wrong question at the wrong time is to operate in unbelief. Many Christians create great obstacles for their faith when they ask the wrong questions at the wrong time.

When you are seeking to know God's plan for your future, you may need to ask Him questions to gain clarity in your spirit of His will. But never question anything that has to do with your redemptive rights.

Healing, peace, joy, provision, freedom from fear, etc., are all your redemptive rights – the things that belong to you because of the price Jesus paid to purchase your redemption from anything that steals, kills, or destroys. These are the things you must never question! If you do, you enter into unbelief, and unbelief is a poor receiver. Questions are the parent of unbelief! The more questions you ask, the further you travel into unbelief.

Eve listened to one question that the serpent offered her in the garden of Eden, *"Hath God said?"* and humanity has suffered for it ever since. The devil offers questions, but God offers answers! Questions are of the mental realm, but answers are of the spirit realm – the faith realm!

When God speaks to us, we must respond correctly if what He says is to be fulfilled. Zachariah responded wrong, and suffered for it. Mary responded right, and blessed humanity!

Through His Word He is speaking to us, and we must respond correctly with words that agree with His words.

For example, 1 Peter 2:24 tells us, *"...by whose stripes ye were healed."* We must respond correctly in the face of symptoms by saying, "God's Word tells me that by the stripes of Jesus I was healed, so I am healed now!" Those words agree with God's words, so He can then bring them to pass in your life.

Those Christians who won't speak words that agree with God's Word which states that they are healed, won't experience healing, although it belongs to them.

There is much that belongs to us, but if we don't respond correctly by speaking the right words, we won't experience those blessings in our own lives. God cannot move for you and in you without your agreement – your correct response.

In fact, no one can be saved unless they respond correctly to the gift of Jesus as their Savior. Jesus belongs to the whole world, but He can only occupy the hearts of those who respond correctly to Him by calling on His Name.

All of God's blessings that belong to you need your correct response before they will be experienced by you. In different experiences I've had with the Lord, I've seen the need for responding correctly.

A VISITATION

I can think of one specific occasion when I was sitting in a chair on our platform leading the congregation in prayer. As I sat praying, Jesus stood to the right side of my chair. I didn't see Him, but I knew by the word of knowledge that He was there. I sat there for about five minutes waiting for Him to speak to me, but He didn't say a word – He just stood there. Finally, I realized that although I knew He was there, I hadn't responded to His presence. So quickly I said, "What have You come to say to me?" When I asked that, He gave me direction for the coming year.

What I want you to see is that He needs correct response, but He won't force Himself on anyone. Some will assume, "Well, if He wants to say something to me, then He can." Well, He won't if He isn't responded to correctly.

I firmly believe that if I had not responded to Him as He stood by my chair during that service, that He would have soon left without saying to me what He came to say.

There's much He has to say to us through His Word and by His Spirit if we'll only listen and respond correctly.

WAITING FOR A RESPONSE

One minister gave an account of a time when he was asleep in a travel trailer while conducting a crusade in a particular city, and he awoke to the sound of the trailer door opening. He got up to see who had come in, yet saw no one. He went back to lie down, and as he did, he sensed that an angel had come into the trailer, and was standing by his bed. In a few minutes he sensed the angel turn and walk away, going out the door of the trailer. Months later Jesus and the angel appeared to the minister, and Jesus reminded the minister of the night the angel had come into his travel trailer. Jesus told him that he hadn't yielded and responded to the angel, so he didn't deliver the message he had; but that if he would respond to the angel, that the angel would again appear to him as the Lord willed, and would give him guidance and direction concerning the things of life.

Again, we see that God may have something for us, but without a correct response from us, we won't receive it.

Responding opens you up to receiving. Without a correct response, there is no receiving.

YOU STILL HAVE TO ASK

It's recorded in Matthew 6:8 that Jesus declared:

...your Father knoweth what things ye have need of, before ye ask him.

Yet, the Bible clearly instructs us to ask for the things we need. James tells us, *"You have not, because you ask not"* (James 4:2).

Someone may ask, "Since He knows I have need of something, why doesn't He just give that to me without having to ask for it?"

The answer to that question is that knowledge doesn't equal permission.

A neighbor may know that you have a car parked in your driveway, but that doesn't mean that the neighbor has your permission to drive the car.

Likewise, God has knowledge of the things that we need, but His knowledge doesn't give Him permission to give that to you. He needs your permission to move in your life, and He gets that permission when you ask Him.

Many sit idly by and wait for God to drop things on them, but that is an incorrect response. He must have your active participation by responding correctly to Him.

BE A REVIVAL!

Too many times we spend our time praying for God to move and manifest Himself by sending revival. But God's not the One who's slow to move. God has never stopped moving. We are the ones who are slow to respond to the movement He's making. He can't move apart from us. Jesus is the head, but we are the body. The head is dependent upon the body to carry out the movement. He's waiting on us to respond to Him; then we will see greater manifestations of His Spirit when we do.

We don't have to talk God into sending a revival. God needs you to be a revival! Smith Wigglesworth stated, "I live full of the Spirit; that's why I have revival everywhere I go."

What did he mean by that? You can't be full of the Spirit if you're not responding to the Spirit on a daily basis. If you'll respond to Him, He'll move through you, and you'll be a revival – manifesting God's plan and power everywhere you go. God will manifest Himself through you. God manifests Himself through those who respond to Him.

We receive from the Spirit of God according to the measure that we respond to Him. We will never receive more than we respond to. If we fail to respond, then we fail to receive.

DON'T HINDER THE SPIRIT

If a husband and wife get into a spat and storm out of the room, deciding not to talk to each other, the husband may later decide that he wants to make amends. He may go over to his wife and put his arms around her shoulders, letting her know that he's ready to put the situation behind them. But if the wife isn't ready for it to be over, she may fold up her arms, clam up and not return any positive response to him. If she does that, the husband will drop his arms, back away and not make any further movement toward her.

Even so, if the Spirit of God moves upon us, but we don't return the proper response in His direction, then He too will stop moving in our direction until He receives a response that invites His movement. Sitting idly by and failing to respond in a positive manner to Him will quench His movement in our lives. He will not move uninvited because He won't violate anyone's will.

We are warned in 1 Thessalonians 5:19 not to quench the Spirit; and again in Ephesians 4:30 we're told not to grieve the Holy Spirit. When we fail to respond to Him, not only do we grieve Him, but we quench Him, hindering Him from moving.

GOD MOVES WITH PURPOSE

When the Spirit of God is moving in an extraordinary way in our services, He's moving that way so that He can accomplish a work. Anything God does carries a purpose with it; He isn't just moving randomly with no plan in mind. He has a purpose He is wanting to accomplish. When the Spirit moves among us, it's to accomplish that purpose. He doesn't just move on us to make us feel something (although His movement can be felt tangibly). There is a purpose in His movement. He will bring revelation, break yokes off lives, heal bodies, and make divine impartations, etc., but a lack of response to His moving will affect what He can accomplish. His purpose is not just so we can say that the anointing felt good, or that it made us run or jump; but there is to be fruit from it – healed bodies, broken bondages, and a host of other blessings. Don't just limit and confine His movement to what you feel when He was moving, but respond to Him so that lasting changes can be made in your life and in the lives of those present.

Whether or not people's needs are met in a service doesn't just depend on the preacher, the sermon, or even on God; but it also depends on and involves the response of the whole congregation to the moving of the Spirit.

SPECTATOR OR PARTICIPATOR?

If you were to attend a professional football game, you would immediately notice the two groups of people present in the stadium – the spectators and the participators. The participators are out on the field applying real effort in the game, and spectators are sitting in the stands enjoying the labors of the participators. One major difference between the spectators and the participators is that the spectators pay to be there, and the participators get paid to be there!

The Bible shows us very definitely that the Holy Spirit has only ever been a participator in the plan of God – He's never been only a spectator.

Genesis 1 tells how the Spirit of God was hovering over the face of the deep waiting for God to speak words. When God did speak, saying, *"Let there be light..."* the Holy Spirit moved with those words and brought them to pass. He was a participator with God!

Since the Holy Spirit lives in every born again believer, and He is each person's Helper, He will never lead us into being simply a spectator. He cannot help the believer to be what He has never been – a spectator! The Holy Spirit will lead every believer into being a participator with God.

Even Jesus' earthly ministry depended upon His obedience to follow and respond to the Holy Spirit. If Jesus' effectiveness depended upon Him responding properly to the Holy Spirit, how can we do any less, and still be effective?

CHAPTER TWO

Following God's Plan

There is a plan to every service that we must flow with if that service is to accomplish God's plan.

If you were standing beside a river, you would see that there is a continual flow to it. But you would also see that it never just flows in a completely straight line. You would see bends in the river, and watch it make subtle, and sometimes drastic, direction changes; but there would still be a continual flow.

To watch the flow of a church service that is moving with the Spirit of God, you will see a service that isn't confined to going just one direction, but several. It may start out with a time of praise and worship, then announcements may be made. Tithes and offerings would be received, then the minister would preach or teach, and end up by giving an altar call.

To respond to the Spirit in the service would involve responding with all those different directions in the service.

When praise and worship is going on, respond by entering in. Don't just stand there holding on to the chair in front of you, or staring at the words to the song without directing your heart to participate. Some congregation members even time a late arrival to church so that they can bypass the praise and worship portion of the service. That isn't responding properly to the Spirit, and it can grieve Him.

If an employee habitually arrived late for work, his boss would know that he is responding wrong to his job and responsibilities; and by not honoring his position, he could be fired.

Well, we have a responsibility, but higher than that — an honor, to respond to the Holy Spirit in a service. It's wrong to treat that honor lightly by not being prompt and not participating in every flow of the service.

As a pastor, it's easy to see that the people who purpose to be late so that they can bypass portions of the service are the most needy people in the church. They always flock to the pastor after a service wanting special prayer, counseling, or just needing attention. But it's difficult to help those people because they don't honor the Spirit of God, the Word, the pastor, or the congregation during a service.

After the praise and worship time of the service, there may be a turn in the flow of the service, and the pastor may receive the tithes and offerings from the people. Again, it's the job of the congregation to respond to the Spirit in this flow. Respond by giving! It's the lack of a proper response during offering time to sit on your wallet, not intending to participate. Even if you don't have any money to give in the offering, don't just sit there! Give a pen, a mint – give something. It's not only about the amount of the money you give, but it's about participating and responding to that flow of the service. Involve yourself in it in whatever way you can.

Your giving opens you up so that you can receive – so, give something! It's not that God only gives to those who are givers; but it's only the givers who have created the capacity to receive. Those who fail to give, fail to create a capacity to receive. So, if God sent provision their way, they wouldn't be able to receive because they haven't created that capacity.

If you have a jar of juice that's only half full, and you wanted to fill it up, you'd have to take the lid off before you could pour more juice in there. If the lid were still on but you tried to pour juice in it anyway, it would just run off the top of the lid; the container couldn't receive it.

That's where some believers are. They want God to pour provision into their life, but they've kept their vessel sealed up by failing to give out. Giving takes the lid off your capacity to receive. When you give, you have taken the lid off your vessel, and you have created a capacity to where something more can be added. So, participate in the flow of giving by giving something!

After the receiving of the tithes and offerings, another turn will be made in the flow of the service, and the pastor will begin to minister the Word. Well, keep responding! Don't just sit looking straight ahead, bare-ly blinking an eye. Respond by participating. Actively take into your spirit what is flowing out of the minister. No, don't out-preach the preacher, but respond with your mouth in a way that is fitting. Don't draw atten-tion to yourself, but respond with your mouth in a way that flows with the service.

Religion will get angry in a service if people shout, "Amen" or "Hallelujah" at the preaching, because reli-gious devils know that if people respond, then they'll receive; and the devil doesn't want anyone receiving anything good.

But it's important that the mouth get involved in responding. The Bible tells us, *"Out of the abundance of the heart, the mouth speaks."* Notice, that when there's an abundance of movement in a man's heart (his spirit), that it starts flowing out into the body, and the mouth picks it up and gets involved. The body of the man will be affected by what's happening in the spirit of man.

You can measure the fullness of a man's spirit by how his mouth is responding. A man will respond to the measure of fullness in his spirit. Some don't respond in a service and call themselves "dignified," when it's really because they're empty.

THE WORD DID NOT PROFIT THEM

I want us to look at a passage in Hebrews 4, but before we do, let me remind you of the setting of this scripture. Paul is reminding us of the journey that

God's people made out of Egypt and through the wilderness, going toward the promised land. They wandered in the wilderness for 40 years because they wouldn't believe and act on God's instructions to them. As a result, many tragedies came to them, and eventually an entire generation had to die off before God could fulfill His Word to them.

Paul says about their unbelief in Hebrews 4:2:

For unto us was the gospel preached, as well as unto them: but THE WORD PREACHED DID NOT PROFIT THEM, not being mixed with faith in them that heard it.

How revealing that scripture is to us. Can you ever hear the Word of God preached and not profit or benefit from it? Absolutely! That happens in every church service. People are present, but they're not benefiting from that Word. Why? Because the Word has to be mixed with something before it will work. What does it have to be mixed with? Faith! But notice, it's not the faith of the preacher being talked about in this passage; it's the faith of the hearer!

How is faith mixed with the Word? Through speaking words that agree with God's Word.

Faith comes by hearing the Word preached, but faith isn't released through hearing the Word preached. Faith is released out of your spirit through speaking words that agree with God's words. Faith comes to your spirit through hearing, but it's released through words. When you hear the Word preached, you believe; when you speak the Word, you receive!

Mix faith with the Word you're hearing in the church services. Come to church expecting to hear from God, and when the preaching of the Word goes forth, God is speaking to you. Respond to it by opening your mouth and saying something! You don't have to shout something, but say something in response.

When the pastor is ministering and God starts authoring some things in your heart, open up your mouth and move with that, saying, "That's it, that's my answer," or "That's it. That's the answer I've been needing." When you respond to what God is doing on the inside of you, then you'll receive more as you act on what you have.

When the Spirit moves in you and upon you through the preaching, respond to that. Don't just sit there making no acknowledgement at all of what God is saying to you. Don't quench the Spirit when He moves on you by not responding.

So many are just in a bad spiritual habit of sitting through a sermon, and giving little or nor response. It's just a bad habit! Some have come out of churches that discouraged any kind of outward response, or some have not been taught. Still others have just been content to be a spectator in the services, watching the participators enjoy themselves. But no one ever got full watching someone else eat! You have to eat! You have to participate! You have to respond! You will have to develop the spiritual habit of responding in your own life. In every service, check yourself to make sure you're responding; then, as you go throughout your daily life, you'll be quick to respond properly as the Spirit guides you in the everyday affairs of life. But the place you're going to learn how to respond is by practicing it in church services.

No, don't do something in a service that draws the people's attention to you, but flow and respond to the Spirit.

Words Open You Up

Words spoken will open up your heart to receive more, so get your mouth involved.

You know that if you're having dinner with some- one who is talking bad about others, and if you ever open your mouth to join them in their wrong conver- sation, their words will go right into you, and you'll become critical like them.

Wrong words spoken will open you up to wrong things. But right words spoken will open you up to right things!

Psalm 81:10 instructs us, *"...open thy mouth wide, and I will fill it."* When you start speaking right things, God can put more into you; a greater measure of blessings will come.

Agree with the Word going forth from your pastor; declare your "Amen" to it. Participate, respond, and get filled up.

After the minister delivers his sermon, he may call for a healing line, inviting those who need healing to come forward. Well, stay hooked on and respond to the

Spirit by flowing with Him. Don't become disinterested in the service or pass notes to your neighbor as the sick are being ministered to. Release your faith on their behalf. How would you want others to respond if you were the one in need of healing? That's an important flow of the service; stay hooked on, and respond by releasing your faith with them.

The pastor may then close out the service by giving an altar call for those who want to be born again. This is not your cue to get up to go to the restroom, pace around in the foyer, or make an early escape from the service to beat the traffic. No, it's still necessary to respond. Be praying for those who come forward. Don't grieve the Spirit by not caring about people receiving God's best for them. Flow and respond with every direction the Spirit of God leads in a service.

Our church services are to be the place where we practice responding to the Spirit so that we'll become proficient at it. It's easier to respond to the Spirit when you're surrounded by other believers who are also responding. Then, you'll know better how to respond to the Spirit when you're at home alone with no one else joining in with you.

The local church is the only place where you will learn how to respond to the Spirit on a continual basis, and to mature in your ability to respond accurately. No one's teaching you how to respond to the Spirit at the mall, at your business office, or the theatre. The local church is where that's taught. Be a good student and learn well, for to finish your race, you're going to need to know how to respond to the Spirit of God.

We must not only respond to the Spirit when we are in a church service, but we must respond to the Spirit in our everyday life.

QUICK TO RESPOND

In looking at the twelve disciples who were with Jesus, Peter stands out as the most mentioned disciple. He had experiences that the other disciples didn't have. His mistakes were recorded more than those of any other disciple, but he also had more successes. Why? Because he responded more than the other disciples. He was usually the first one to make movement in a new direction. He was the only disciple to step out of the boat and walk on water. He was the first one to stand up and preach to multitudes when coming out of the upper room, filled with the Holy Ghost. He was the first one to preach the Gospel to the Gentiles at Cornelius' house.

Those who are quick to respond to the Spirit are also the ones who are quick to receive, and those who are most likely to be used by the Spirit.

It's important to not hesitate to respond to the Spirit when He's moving. You know yourself that you can't steer a parked car. The car has to move so it can be directed. Neither can God steer a non-responsive person; they must respond to Him so He can direct them.

In a church that's dry and void of the moving of the Spirit, no one is responding to the Spirit. They have no idea that they play a role in receiving from God;

they think it's all up to God and the preacher to do something.

CHAPTER THREE

Spiritual Hunger

During Brother Hagin's crusade in our church, we had dinner with him in the back room after the services, and he began talking to us about the gifts of the Spirit manifesting in our services.

He told of ministering in churches where the gifts of the Spirit operated freely; then going to other churches where there was no operation of the gifts of the Spirit.

In one particular church where there were no gifts of the Spirit in operation, the pastor told Brother Hagin, "I don't know why we don't have the gifts of the Spirit operating, because we've prayed for them to operate."

Brother Hagin answered, "The gifts of the Spirit don't operate because we pray; they operate because the people are hungry for them." Then Brother Hagin went on to quote to us 1 Corinthians 12:31, "...*covet earnestly the best gifts...*" and 1 Corinthians 14:1, "*...DESIRE spiritual gifts...*"

" 'Covet' and 'desire' are words that show hunger," Brother Hagin continued. "We must teach the people to be hungry. That's the key to having miracles – hunger!"

A hungry man will respond differently at the dinner table than a satisfied man. A hungry man will forget his manners. He will be quick to respond to the food that's on the table. He won't eat only the food that's on his plate, but he will even eat the leftovers that others leave behind.

Spiritually, we must be so hungry for the movement of the Holy Spirit that we will be quick to respond to what He is serving us in a meeting.

A hungry man will even eat food that he doesn't like; he doesn't sit at the table and act picky. But a satisfied man will let food pass him by until he's served something he likes. You can tell who's hungry and who's satisfied by how they act at the dinner table.

Proverbs 27:7 tells us:

The full soul loatheth an honeycomb; but to the hungry soul every bitter thing is sweet.

The hungry man will even eat something that doesn't taste good – his hunger compels him to, but a satisfied man rejects even the sweet things that are put before him.

Someone who is spiritually hungry doesn't just respond to words that are easy to hear, but he will respond to correction or rebuke, and he'll be thankful to eat them. But a satisfied man will push the dish of correction or rebuke from him, rejecting anything that doesn't agree with his taste. Our response level shows our hunger level.

We are to come to church expecting to receive from God, expecting to hear the answer we may need, expecting to receive the strength of the Word into our spirits.

Expectant people act differently than non-expectant people. Some believe that their attendance in church is enough; they think that their spiritual duties are fulfilled just by their presence in the service, but they will never receive from God beyond their own response.

How to Attend Church

It's good to attend church, but there are many Christians who attend church, and still fail in life. It's *how* you attend church that makes all the difference. While getting dressed before a service, declare within yourself, "When I get to church, I'm going to receive the answers I need to hear. The Word of God and the power of God are going to move mightily in me and make a difference in my life!" While in the car driving to the service, thank God for what He's going to do in the lives of those present in the service.

Church services are to be the place where drastic changes are made in people's lives – expect that to happen! Before you even arrive at church, begin to · respond in faith to what God is going to do during the service. Make a demand on God's power with your faith. Don't wait for the service to start before you start responding and releasing your faith through speaking expectant words.

ENHANCING THE ATMOSPHERE

Door greeters and ushers are not just "hand-shakers" and "bucket-passers." They are to create an expectancy with their words to the people coming into the church building.

You never know what difficulties, situations, and hardships people may be facing when they walk through the church doors. They may be facing a tragic situation, and the greeter can make all the difference by speaking words of expectancy like, "God has answers for your life today; expect to hear them in the service this morning." Words like that not only bless the one who says them, but they can cause expectancy to rise in the heart of that one who may be troubled. If people will be expectant, then they'll respond to what God is doing in the service. Motivate others to respond!

When the service begins, we need to be the first ones to start responding and drawing on God for His plan to come to pass in that service.

On one occasion, when Jesus appeared to Kenneth Hagin, He told Brother Hagin that He has a plan for every service. With that being the case, we shouldn't settle for anything less than His plan coming to pass in a service. But His plan won't just come to pass simply because He has a plan, it comes to pass because faith is exercised. It's not just up to the minister to desire God's plan to come to pass in the service, but it's also the congregation's responsibility to participate, respond, and exercise faith by being expectant.

In the service, don't wait for someone else to stir you up. The Bible instructs us to stir ourselves up (2 Timothy 1:6)! Don't wait till the service begins before you start stirring yourself up; stir yourself up before you even arrive at the church.

In responding, don't do that which would distract from the service and draw attention to yourself, but respond in a manner that adds to the service and doesn't take away from it.

IT'S NOT ABOUT US!

Many hesitate to respond in a service because they're so self-conscious that they're wondering what those around them will think. One thing must be understood – the service is not about us – it's about God getting *His* way! If people don't respond because they're too self-conscious, then God won't get His way, and people won't receive the things they need. It's wrong to be more mindful of ourselves than of God. When we fail to respond to the way God is moving in a service, it's because we're thinking about ourselves, and not about Him.

DON'T GRIEVE THE SPIRIT

I was conducting a service where I started calling out healings by the word of knowledge. I had called out about four different physical conditions that God said someone present had. Those people raised their hands to say that the words of knowledge given described their conditions. I ministered to them, then continued to call out another condition in someone's body; yet no one responded. I continued to ask the congregation who had that condition, and even gave more details of what the symptoms were in their body. Still, no one responded.

I then called out another condition that someone else was experiencing, but again, no one responded. I continued to tell more details about their condition, and still, no one responded. At that point, the anointing lifted and I received no more words of knowledge of healings.

Shortly thereafter the service ended, and I started to leave the building. As I approached the door, two different ladies came up to me and said that I had called out their physical conditions exactly but they didn't want to come forward, and asked if I would pray for their healing.

I questioned them, "Why didn't you respond when I called out your condition during the service?" Both of them answered, "I was too embarrassed to come forward."

People can be so preoccupied with themselves that they will pass up God's blessing for them.

Blind Bartimaeus wanted to be healed more than he wanted to guard his dignity. He cried out so loud that the crowd told him to shut up, but he just cried louder. His reward was total healing.

If you're not careful, you can hold onto your human dignity and let go of God's blessings!

Did I minister to those two ladies who stopped me before I left the building? Yes, but that stronger anointing had lifted off of me, and they didn't receive all they could have received if they had responded at the time the Spirit of God was moving in the service.

The most disappointing thing about that situation is that there were others present who needed healing, and could have been healed. But those two ladies who failed to respond correctly to the Spirit when He gave the word of knowledge grieved Him, so He quit moving that way.

When we fail to respond properly in a service, it's not just us we affect, but others who need what God has for them.

JESUS GOT A WRONG RESPONSE

In Jesus' hometown of Nazareth, there were people present who needed to be healed, who could have been healed, and who should have been healed; but because others responded wrong to Jesus, He was unable to do for them what He came to do (Mark 6).

People think that God can do anything He wants, any time He wants, but they are mistaken. Mark 6:5 tells us that in His own hometown, Jesus, *"...could there do no mighty work..."*

For God to get His way, people must cooperate with Him. If they don't cooperate by responding correctly, they won't receive what God has for them.

Religion falls back on the thinking that God is sovereign and can do whatever He wants, anytime He wants.

God is sovereign in heaven. Everything in heaven is in line with His perfect will. But He's not sovereign on the earth unless people will cooperate with Him. On the earth, God is confined to working through His body – the body of Christ.

When God put Adam in the garden of Eden, he gave Adam the authority over the earth.

Genesis 1:28 tells us:

And God blessed them, and God said unto them, Be fruitful, and multiply, and replenish the earth, and SUBDUE it: and have DOMINION...

If God would have been the One exercising His authority on the earth, Satan would never have gotten into the Garden of Eden and enticed Adam to sin. Satan got into that garden because Adam failed to exercise the authority given him by God over the enemy.

When Adam sinned and yielded to Satan, then Satan assumed the authority upon the earth. That's why there has been great tragedy in the earth since the time of Adam.

2 Corinthians 4:4 calls Satan *"...the god of this world..."* When did he become the god of this world? When Adam handed his own authority over to him.

But Jesus came and spoiled principalities and powers (Colosians 2:15), and broke Satan's power over those who would receive Jesus as their Lord. God raised us up together with Christ in heavenly places. Our bodies are still on this earth, but in our authority we are seated with Christ. Our authority stems from our being seated with Christ. God restored to the church what Adam lost to Satan. Therefore, for God to work His plan in the earth, He must have our cooperation.

If God were sovereign on the earth, there would be nothing to harm or destroy on the earth. But there is coming a day when Satan will be chained up and cast out of the earth. Until that time, we must continue to exercise our authority to keep Satan from carrying out his plans against our lives.

When we respond to God, then we invite Him and enable Him to fulfill His plan in the earth. But when we fail to respond properly to Him, we hinder Him from bringing His plan to pass in the earth.

When Jesus was on the earth, God worked His plan through Jesus. But now God is working His plan through the body of Christ, the church. That's why it's so important that we cooperate with and respond to God.

When we fail to respond properly to the Spirit of God, we're the ones who lose out. What we don't respond properly to, we'll lose.

Anyone who ended up in the divorce court is there because somebody in that marriage quit responding right in the marriage, and the union was lost. If we are to hold to the good things we receive, we must respond correctly to them.

The Bible tells us that when the Word is sown into someone's heart, the devil comes immediately to steal it away. But if someone responds to that Word by acting on it, the enemy can't steal it from them. If the Word is responded to, they won't lose it. What you don't respond properly to, you will lose.

CHAPTER FOUR

Improper Response

Let's look at some instances in the Word where people didn't respond properly to Jesus.

Matthew 11:20-24 reads,

> *Then began he* (Jesus) *to upbraid the cities wherein most of his mighty works were done, because they repented not:*

> *Woe unto thee, Chorazin! woe unto thee, Bethsaida! for if the mighty works, which were done in you, had been done in Tyre and Sidon, they would have repented long ago in sackcloth and ashes.*

> *But I say unto you, It shall be more tolerable for Tyre and Sidon at the day of judgment, than for you.*

> *And thou Capernaum, which art exalted unto heaven, shalt be brought down to hell: for if the mighty works, which have been done in thee,*

had been done in Sodom, it would have remained until this day.

But I say unto you, That it shall be more tolerable for the land of Sodom in the day of judgment, than for thee.

Why does He say that Capernaum had been singled out as having been exalted unto heaven?

Not only were mighty miracles done in Capernaum, but Jesus had set up His ministry headquarters there. Capernaum was the city hosting the Messiah, yet they did not respond properly to Him.

So, Jesus singled out three cities who were in line for judgment: Chorazin, Bethsaida, and Capernaum. Up until this time, mighty works of power and miracles had been worked in their midst through the Son of God. But once Jesus pronounced judgment on them, He never worked another miracle in those cities.

We can see proof of that judgment in Mark 8:22-26:

And he (Jesus) *cometh to Bethsaida* (remember that Bethsaida was one of the three cities that Jesus pronounced judgment on)*; and they bring a blind man unto him, and besought him to touch him.*

And he (Jesus) *took the blind man by the hand, and LED HIM OUT OF THE TOWN...*

Why did Jesus lead the blind man out of the town? Because Jesus had pronounced judgment on the city, and He worked no more miracles in that city from that time on. If this man was to receive his healing, he was going to have to be outside that city.

WHERE YOU CAN'T RECEIVE

Did you know that there are some places where a person can't receive healing? Where Jesus isn't honored as the Healer, no one will be healed there.

Being in a place that doesn't honor the Word or honor Jesus as the Healer, will keep the sick from receiving healing.

If they are to be healed, they must separate themselves from that place.

Jesus wanted this blind man to be healed, but for that to happen He had to get him out of the wrong place, and away from those who didn't honor Him.

Did you know that if you seek out your fellowship among those who don't honor the Word, it will hinder you from receiving what you need from God? Their unbelief will affect you.

There have been many times when someone will attend one of our services who is in need of healing, but belongs to a church that doesn't teach on or believe in healing. They realize they can't get healed in their church, so they go to a different place when they need healing. In our services they will get healed, but if they return to their own church that doesn't believe in it, they will end up losing their healing. Why is that? When they surround themselves with those who don't believe in healing, the unbelief of others will charge the atmosphere with unbelief. The words of doubt from others will attack their faith, and they'll talk them out of their healing. Plus, if they're to maintain the healing they've received, they have to keep feeding their faith concerning the subject of healing, and their faith won't get fed in a place that doesn't believe in it.

When you're believing God for healing, you had better make sure you surround yourself with people of faith; not people who question and doubt God's Word.

Whether you know it or not, your spirit and your faith is affected by those you fellowship with and by those you surround yourself with.

A FAMILY'S UNBELIEF

Years ago, a man was in one of our services who was diagnosed with AIDS, and was dying of cancer and tuberculosis. He was on an oxygen tank, confined to a wheelchair, and unable to walk on his own. He also had been unable to eat on his own for some time. But in our service, when my husband laid his hands on him, he felt the healing anointing go into him. By the Spirit, my husband then gave him instructions, telling him to come back to the next service and to testify of his healing. The man said he would.

For the next couple of days, after being prayed for, the man was able to walk around on his own, eat solid food, and was taken off the oxygen tank. He had made a remarkable improvement that had even amazed his nurse.

But at the time of the next service, when he was to come back to the church and testify, family members talked him out of going to church, saying, "It's cold outside and you could catch pneumonia. You'd better not go!" (When you've been diagnosed with AIDS, cancer and tuberculosis, and told you've only got days to live, what kind of threat is pneumonia to you?)

But they convinced him to stay home, and a few days later, he was dead.

Although he had a miraculous turnaround, he lost it by listening to those around him, instead of obeying the man of God who told him to come back to church and testify. The atmosphere he was in was charged with unbelief, and it killed him!

When you're believing God for something, you have to guard your fellowship and the words you hear.

If Jesus was to get His blind man healed, He was going to have to get him out of that city!

The account of Jesus ministering to the blind man continues in Mark 8:23:

> *And he* (Jesus) *took the blind man by the hand, and led him out of the town; and when he had spit on his eyes, and put his hands upon him, he asked him if he saw aught.*
>
> *And he looked up, and said, I see men as trees, walking.*
>
> *After that he put his hands again upon his eyes, and made him look up: and he was restored, and saw every man clearly.*

This is the only account in Jesus' earthly ministry where He ministered to the same person more than once. It had nothing to do with the anointing or the degree of power being less upon Jesus at this time. It had to do with the blind man's ability to receive. Since this man had been fellowshipping with those in a city that rejected Jesus, it affected the blind man's ability to receive healing, even with God's own Son ministering to him personally and privately.

Many Christians don't realize the effect that wrong fellowship has on their spiritual strength and well-being.

Always guard closely your own fellowship, and the fellowship of your family. At a time of testing, when your faith life is most important for you, you want to make sure you've made the right investments in your fellowship.

FOUNDATIONS REVEALED

Remember the parable Jesus spoke in Matthew 7:24-27 about the house built on the sand, and the one built on the rock. The same storm came to both houses. The house built on the rock wasn't exempt from the storm, but its outcome was different from the one built on the sand.

The house built on the sand had a great fall, while the house built on the rock remained strong.

The problem wasn't the storm. If the storm had been the problem, it would have been able to destroy both homes. The problem was the foundation upon which the house was built. It was the storm that revealed the foundation of both houses, not the calm. In the good weather, the foundations of the houses appeared to be the same; they both appeared to be good and strong. But the storm told the real story; it showed up the weakness of the house that fell.

This parable isn't just about two houses – it's about two lives! The storms of life will come and beat on every man – no man is exempt from the storms of life. But the man who builds his life on the rock by being a doer of the Word, will still be standing strong when the storm has passed on.

Another important point to see about this parable is that what a man does prior to a storm determines his outcome. Many wait until the storm hits before they start building the Word in them, but sometimes they can start too late. It's best to use the calm prior to the storm for your construction time.

FELLOWSHIPPING IN THE WRONG PLACE

This blind man had created an additional difficulty in his life by fellowshipping in a community that didn't honor Jesus. It affected his ability to receive fully when first ministered to. Only because Jesus kept working with him was he able to be fully healed.

Yet, we do see Jesus giving the man some crucial instructions after he was healed.

And he (Jesus) *sent him away to his house, saying, Neither go into the town, nor tell it to any in the town.*

(Mark 8:26)

Notice, Jesus sent him back home, but said not to go back into that town. So, his home must not have been in that town. He lived in one place, but made his fellowship in another place! Don't fellowship in a place where you shouldn't be.

If this man was to keep his healing, he had to stay out of that town of wrong fellowship.

Fellowshipping in the wrong place can cost you your healing. Fellowshipping with wrong people can cause you to lose the blessing of God on your life.

When God delivers you, you had better make sure you don't go back to the same places where you had your fellowship of sin. Don't even go near the location. Don't go back to find your fellowship there, or you'll lose your blessing. This is what Jesus was warning this man about.

But Jesus gave him even further instruction, "...*Neither go into the town, NOR TELL IT to any in the town.*"

Why would Jesus instruct the blind man to not go back to even testify to his healing in that town? Because Jesus had already pronounced judgment on that town, and therefore, no more miracles would be worked there.

They had rejected Him there, therefore, they were unable to *receive* anything from Him.

It's not that God is unable to give anything to those who reject Him, but they are unable to receive anything from God if they reject Him. The failure is not on God's end, but on theirs.

GUARD YOUR BLESSINGS

This instruction Jesus gave the blind man about not telling the people in the town of Bethsaida of his healing is in line with another statement Jesus made which is recorded in Matthew 7:6:

Give not that which is holy unto the dogs, neither cast ye your pearls before swine, lest they trample them under their feet, and turn again and rend you.

What is meant by Jesus calling someone a "swine"? If we look at how a swine would behave, we can see what He meant.

You could walk into a pig's pen and lay a newspaper down in front of him and tell him, "Piggy, this newspaper is what men say about today's events and people. The actions of men are recorded here; but this whole newspaper will change tomorrow. Different events and different people will be recorded about tomorrow."

Then you could take a Bible and lay it out on the ground right next to that newspaper and explain to the pig, "Now, this Bible is the holy Word of God. In this book is recorded God's Word, thoughts, and actions. This Word will not change tomorrow. It will be the same forever; it will never change. This Word will take a man's life and set it on course."

After your instruction to that pig, he will take the newspaper, step on it, roll around on it, and perhaps chew on it for a little while. He would then go over to the Bible and treat it the exact same way. He would stomp on it, roll over on it, and chew it for a while. Why? Because he's a swine! Nothing holds any value to him. He doesn't know anything about honor. There's nothing honorable in him that causes him to treat what's valuable and precious with respect and reverence. The Word is no different to him than the newspaper. He won't treat one thing more honorably than another thing.

That's what Jesus was referring to in Matthew 7:6 when He said:

> *Give not that which is holy to the dogs, neither cast ye your pearls before swine.*

They won't treat anything with honor or reverence. They will mishandle that which is precious and priceless.

Jesus was saying that some people are the same way as these animals; they mishandle and dishonor what is precious and priceless. If you lay it before them, they will either reject it or mishandle it, so, don't give it to them. These things are to be honored and valued, not cast before those who know nothing of honor.

This isn't referring to those who are lost and need to hear the Gospel. But it's referring to those who have heard the Gospel, and mishandle it through their rejection of it.

The mighty works that Jesus did were mishandled and rejected in the three cities that He pronounced judgment on, so He was hindered from blessing them because of their dishonor of Him.

Notice what is further stated in Matthew 7:6 in connection with not casting your pearls before swine. *"...lest they trample them under their feet, and turn again and rend you."* If you cast your precious things before a dishonorable person who rejects it, they'll even turn on you and attack you. They won't rejoice at your healing. They won't rejoice at your prosperity. They won't rejoice with you about an answered prayer. They'll mock you and scoff at it. They'll treat that priceless thing dishonorably. Don't give it to them to dishonor.

This is what Jesus was telling the man who was healed of blindness, "Don't even tell them about your healing in that city." Why? Because they've already shown themselves to be dishonorable by rejecting Jesus and the works He did there previously, and judgment has been pronounced on them.

Cherish and protect that which the Lord has blessed you with. Don't give it over to scoffers who will say they don't believe in that "healing stuff" or that "faith junk." If you don't protect it, you'll lose it. That's what Jesus was warning that man of that day.

THE DANGER OF OFFENSE

Even in Jesus' hometown of Nazareth, He was rejected by that community, and was unable to fulfill God's will in that city.

God's will is that every sick person be healed, that every bound person be made free, that every tormented person live in peace. But when people don't respond properly to God, God is unable to bless them the way He wants to.

When Jesus went to His hometown of Nazareth, the people refused to believe Him and to receive Him as God's Son, and Mark 6:3 tells us, *"...And they were OFFENDED at him."* Offense is a poor receiver. No matter how great someone's need is, offense will shut down and close off their ability to receive anything from God.

Many believers don't realize the great danger they enter into if they get into offense with their spouse, another family member, their boss, a co-worker, a neighbor, or anyone else. Offense is dangerous, for it robs from those who harbor it.

In Mark 6:4, Jesus tells us why they were offended at Him.

> *...A prophet is not without HONOUR, but in his own country, and among his own kin, and in his own house.*

Jesus is letting us know how offense got into them – they didn't honor Him. What you don't honor will end up offending you.

God instructs us about honor in His Word. He tells us to honor God, honor authority, honor our parents, honor those who have the rule over us (anyone who is in authority over you), honor the brethren, and honor all men. Honor is meant to protect us. If we honor someone, then we won't be offended at them. But those we fail to honor will easily offend us if the opportunity arises; and if offense gets into a man's heart, it won't live confined – it will spread like a disease throughout every arena of his life.

In Nazareth, we see a community that failed to honor Jesus, so they became offended at Him. But it doesn't stop there.

Mark 6:5 & 6 tells us:

> *And he* (Jesus) *could there do no mighty work, save that he laid his hands upon a few sick folk, and healed them* (the only ones He was able to help were those with minor ailments). *And he marveled because of their UNBELIEF.*

This passage doesn't tell us that He *wouldn't* do a mighty work there, but that He *couldn't*!

The lack of honor they had toward Him opened the door for them to become offended with Him, and unbelief was the result. Then, because they were in unbelief, there were no mighty works done there. If unbelief hindered Him then, unbelief will hinder Him now.

Notice the three things that operate together: dishonor, offense, unbelief. What begins in dishonor, will graduate to offense, and unbelief will be the end result, which creates an inability to receive anything from God.

The wrong response of the people in the city of Nazareth put them outside the reach of God's power. God couldn't do what He wanted to do for them because they responded wrongly to Him.

Many people have thought, "If Jesus would just appear to me and minister to me, then I would be healed." No, that is not true. These people in His own hometown saw Him with their own eyes, but still wouldn't receive from Him. If someone won't believe Him when they can't see Him, then they wouldn't believe Him if they could see Him.

When the woman with the issue of blood pressed through the multitude to touch the hem of Jesus' garment, she was the only one healed. The multitude was pressing on Him; they were seeing and touching Him, but still, they weren't healed.

It's not enough to see Him or touch Him – you must act on His Word! Seeing Jesus isn't your answer, but acting on His Word is! Receiving what He says is always the right response!

CHAPTER FIVE

Yielding to Your Spirit

Romans 6:12-14 instructs us:

Let not sin therefore reign in your mortal body, that you should obey it in the lusts thereof. Neither yield ye your members as instruments of unrighteousness unto sin: but YIELD yourselves unto God, as those that are alive from the dead, and (yield) *your members as instruments of righteousness unto God.*

For sin shall not have dominion over you...

Whether sin or righteousness reigns in your life is determined by which one you yield to. If you yield to sin, then sin will gain the upper hand; but if you yield to righteousness, then that is what will reign.

Another word for "yield" is "respond." If we "yield" to sin, we're "responding" to sin. We're instructed to not cooperate with sin, but to "yield" to righteousness, or to "respond" to righteousness.

What you're "yielding" to is what you're "responding" to.

The whole Christian walk is one of yielding or responding. The outcome of a man's life is the result of what he responds to every day.

We're to respond to divine love instead of unforgiveness, offense, anger, or bitterness. We're to respond to faith instead of fear and unbelief. We're to respond to patience instead of impatience. We're to respond to joy instead of depression – and the list goes on.

All these good things, love, faith patience, joy, are resident in the spirit of the born again believer, and they must be responded to if they are going to flow out.

Your life is simply a picture, an outflow, of what you're responding to.

Always remember that resident in the flesh of man is every ingredient to bring about failure, but in the spirit of the believer is every ingredient, ability, and power to ensure success. Whether you fail or succeed in this Christian walk is determined by what you choose to respond to – the flesh or the spirit.

Galatians 5:16 instructs us:

This I say then, Walk in the Spirit, and ye shall not fulfil the lust of the flesh.

The word "walk" in this context refers to your manner of living. Live everyday by responding to your spirit within you, which has been born again and now contains the life of God, and then you won't respond to the flesh, for that will bring about failure and cause you to miss the mark.

Can a believer fail? Yes, if he fails to respond to his born-again spirit that is within him.

The reason more people don't receive from God is because they are responding to the wrong things; they aren't responding to the greater One who is in them, in their spirit.

YOUR ANSWER IS IN YOU

Proverbs 20:5 reads:

Counsel in the heart of man is like deep water; but a man of understanding will draw it out.

As a pastor, people will come to me for counseling, for they have questions and are looking for answers. If good counsel is given, those questions are met with answers. So, to receive counsel would mean to receive answers.

We could rightly read Proverbs 20:5 like this:

COUNSEL (or ANSWERS) *in the heart of a man is like deep water; but a man of understanding will draw it* (the answer) *out.*

The Holy Spirit is also called the "Counselor" (John 14:16, The Amplified Bible). What does it mean to say that the Holy Spirit is our Counselor? It means that He is our "answer-giver." When faced with a question or difficulty, we can look to this great Counselor within and He will enlighten us with the answer.

No matter what situation or difficulty you may be facing, your answer is in you, for the "answer-giver" (the Holy Spirit) is *in* you! The greater One is in you! The answer in you is greater than the problem around you!

Since this is true, then why are so many believers living such difficult, problem-filled lives? They are not "responding" to the greater One, the "answer-giver" that is in them. They are running around getting everyone else's opinion on their problem; they're laying in bed at night trying to "figure-out" their answer, and have not received of the Helper who has been in them all along.

Remember what we read in Proverbs 20:5?

Counsel (or answers) *in the heart of a man is like deep water; but a man of understanding* (a man who understands that the answer is in him) *will draw it out.*

Believers fail unnecessarily because they don't understand that the answer is in them. They are looking for help from without instead of from within. They're looking for someone else to pray for them. They are looking for someone else to do the believing for them. Consequently, they aren't responding to the Holy Spirit who is within them; they are responding to things outwardly and things in the natural, so they don't receive their needed help.

Many try in vain to get God to pour out or send something down from heaven that will change their situation, because they have failed to realize that their help is within them; the Holy Spirit is within them.

Any Christian who died prematurely of sickness died with healing in them, for the Healer was in them! Any Christian who failed financially, failed with the Provider in them!

Proverbs 20:5 states:

> *Counsel* (or answers) *in the heart of a man is like deep water; but a man of understanding* (a man who understands that the answer is in him) *will DRAW IT* (the answer) *OUT.*

Realize this: you don't receive in life according to what's in you, you receive in life according to what you draw out of you!

Men of stalwart faith, like Smith Wigglesworth, John G. Lake, Dr. Lester Sumrall and Kenneth Hagin, didn't have anything more in them than you have in you – they just *drew out* more!

If you put a 100-pound man next to a 250-pound weight-lifter, the 100-pound man couldn't say, "Well, he's got more muscles than me." No, they have the exact same number of muscles in their bodies, but the weight-lifter just developed his; and since he developed them, he was able to use them and accomplish things that the 100-pound man couldn't.

The same thing is true spiritually. A believer who fails doesn't fail because he lacks spiritual ability, he fails because he fails to develop the spiritual ability he possesses. It's not an issue of what you possess, but rather, how much you develop what you do possess!

These men of stalwart faith knew what was in them, and they developed what was in them through exercising their spirits. They responded to their spirits. They drew out their great spiritual strength to bring blessing to others.

You draw out the great wealth of the greater One who is in you by two ways:

    1.   Through what you say

    2.   Through what you do, your actions

Isaiah 12:3 reads:

Therefore with joy shall ye DRAW WATER OUT of the wells of salvation.

It's recorded in John 4:14 that Jesus stated:

But whosoever drinketh of the water that I shall give him shall never thirst; but the water that I shall give him shall be IN HIM A WELL OF WATER springing up into everlasting life.

Jesus states that this well of living water – the well of salvation – is in you.

Again, Isaiah said that:

Therefore with joy shall YE DRAW OUT of the well of salvation.

Your salvation is in you – your help is in you. That's why it's with joy, and also a joy, to draw out of the well of salvation – the living water – that's in you; because that's where your help is – your help is in you. Your answer is in you. The Kingdom of God is within you.

Is it any wonder that James 1:2 instructs us to :

...count it all JOY when ye fall into divers temptations...

When you speak in joy and act in line with joy when faced with tests, trials, and temptations, you are drawing out your help from the well of salvation that's in you. When you understand that help and answers are within you to every test and trial of life, you can act and live in joy, no matter how serious the circumstances may seem.

If you fail to act and speak in joy at those times, it's because you have forgotten the One who is within you. If you're troubled by the circumstances around you and the attacks upon you, it's because you've forgotten that the greater One is within you – you've forgotten the great well of salvation that's in you.

Remind yourself of the One who is within you and of His ability within you, and respond to Him. Respond by rejoicing in the face of all opposition. The sooner you get into joy, the sooner your answers will flow out of the well of salvation from within you.

James instructed us that we were to count it all joy when faced with difficulties, because he knew that we won't come out of them until we get into joy. Since the answer is in us, we can rejoice in the Lord – which is an outflow of joy.

DRAWING OUT OF THE WELL

When I was young, my family lived in a small town in Southwest Oklahoma called Olustee. Our city water was what we called "jip water." When you took a drink, it was so full of a metallic taste that it tasted like you were sucking on a nail. Needless to say, we didn't drink it often.

But down the street from our house was a neighbor who had a well of water in her yard. That water tasted so pure. She made the offer to us to come and draw out water as often as we wanted.

When we went to her well, we didn't just stand there looking at the water, wondering why we didn't have any. It would have done no good to fall down by that well and cry, "I need water! I need water!" All we had to do to get it was let down the bucket and draw it out.

Likewise, it does no good to fall on your knees and cry, "I need answers! I need answers!" Just open your mouth and with joy start declaring that what God said in His Word is yours! Draw out your answers from within you by declaring what belongs to you.

Healing is yours. Peace is yours. Provision is yours. Wisdom is yours. Power is yours. All of God's blessings are yours, for Ephesians 1:3 declares:

> *Blessed be the God and Father of our Lord Jesus Christ, who HATH BLESSED US WITH ALL SPIRITUAL BLESSINGS in heavenly places in Christ.*

Another translation reads:

...who has blessed us with everything that heaven itself enjoys...

What we must do is declare what is ours because of His full supply that is within us, and this causes it to flow out. Start drawing out all that is within you. Respond to what's in you!

Paul told Timothy to *stir up* the gift of God that was in him (2 Timothy 1:6). Get that which is in you moving! Get it moving toward your circumstances and needs, and enjoy the supply from the well of salvation.

Actually, every spiritual thing, which is resident in your spirit, must be stirred. Your tongue is the mixer that "stirs up" that living water God has put on the inside of you, and gets it moving in your life. Declare what belongs to you because you're in Him, and rejoice in Him.

Boldly declare, "Life is in me, healing is in me, provision is in me, wisdom is in me, my answers are in me, and they are moving in my life now!"

Someone may ask, "How long do I have to say it?"

Well, when we were drawing water out of the neighbor's well, we didn't just tug on the rope once and then wonder why we didn't have the water. We just kept pulling that rope over and over until the water came spilling over to the top.

How long do you have to declare what's yours? How long do you have to rejoice? 'Till it gets to the top and spills over into those situations in your life.

Respond to the well of life that's in you, and live full!